My Spiritual Thoughts & Words of Remembrance

DEMETRAI L. JOHNSON

ISBN-10: 0985407077
ISBN-13: 978-0-9854070-7-0

DEDICATION

*My Spiritual Thoughts is dedicated to God
my Father, Jesus my Lord and Savior, and
the Holy Spirit my Comforter.*

Words of Remembrance is dedicated to the following people:

Great-Grandmother Mattie Reynolds
June 1894 – March 23, 1994

Uncle Michael L. Johnson
October 1955 - June 18, 2005

Sister Cindy Stacy Shelton
August 1974 – November 23, 2005

Father Larry D. Stacy
September 1952 - March 16, 1998

Desiree C. Stinson
July 2006 – August 6, 2006

CONTENTS

ACKNOWLEDGMENTS

I would like to thank my Heavenly Father for
blessing me with the gift of writing.

I would like to also thank all those who have supported
me; and have taken an interest in
my writings throughout my life.

Gary Crump, Dee Cathey, and Susana Melendez thank
you for taking the time to help me with editing.

My Spiritual Thoughts

MY GOD

My God is everywhere,
When I'm in trouble
He's always there.

My God is always around
He's never let me down
That's why He wears the crown.

My God gave me eyes to see
But I'll still let Him lead me on,
He gave me ears so that I can hear
And learn right from wrong.

My God is everywhere,
When I'm in trouble
He is always there.

My God is always around
He's never let me down
That's why he wears the crown.

HEAVEN

Come and go with me to the world of my Father,
You'll have a wonderful time, with no one to bother.

It's a bright and fun place I know you'll enjoy it,
You don't have to worry, I know you will fit.

Everybody in this world are angels with wings,
This world is Heaven and it's full with everything.

LORD, I'M CALLING FOR YOU

I woke up one morning with a funny feeling,
A funny feeling that something is going to happen.
I got on my knees and closed my eyes
So I can say a prayer,
I called on my God, My Father Cause I know how
much He cares.

Lord I'm calling for you.

Lord I'm calling for you this morning to get
some protection
Just in case something happens.
I want to be with you
Every night and everyday,
So take my mind, body, and soul
And show me the way.

Lord I'm calling for you.

Show me the way you want to me go
I'll be sure to follow,
Order my step and direct my path
Strengthen my walk as I grow.

Lord I'm calling for you.

You're my Father,
You're my God,
We'll never part,
Cause you are always in my heart.

Lord I'm Calling for You.

RISE AGAIN

It was the 4th year BC when Jesus Christ was born
As our savior to be,
He cast out demons, healed the sick & blind but yet you
Said it wasn't He.

He was the Son of God, the Lord of All,
Who had the whole world in His hand.
The day you tried to crucify Him
He knew He would rise again.

You drove nails through His hands and feet
And poked His head with a crown made of thorn,
You hung Him on a wooden cross in the hot blazing sun
As you stood and watched Him until He was gone.

He gave up His life, was crucified, dead and buried
To save us from our sin,
On the third day He rose from the dead
And today He will rise again.

EASTER

Everlasting love is He,
Again He rose
Spiritually.
Taking away our every sin,
Enjoy the presence of His
Radiant soul for which we keep within.

I LOVE HE

I love He
Who takes care of me,
Takes the time to:
**Listen, talk, understand,
comfort and love me,**
Yes!! I did say love me!

He loves me, for who I am,
The beauty of my
insides as well as out.
He loved me from the time
of my birth,
It was only He
I knew nothing about.

Growing up I've learned.
Hey!! I love Him too!
For the love and joy He
gives to me,
And the other things He
doesn't do.

He doesn't:
Interrupt me when
I talk to Him
Corrupts my life.. No!!
He sets me free

He doesn't:
Lust for my love…
And I not for His
We have that spiritual love
That's what it is.

He doesn't:
Lie, cheat, disrespect,
Nor does He deceive me;
For I'm receiving
**Love, Strength,
Faith, Joy and Blessings**
As I'm being
watched by Him.

I love He
Who takes care of me,
Restores my soul
He sets me free.
He's my Lord, and Jesus
Christ
He's my All Mighty.

I love He,
Who takes care of me.

HEART BEAT

When our heart beats
It beats for the love of Jesus Christ,
Lord our Father God
For He's always with us.

Our heart beats for the love of joy
He brings to our hearts,
To lift us up when things
Go wrong and fall apart.

Our heart beats for His strength
He gives us to continue to live;
Through our day to day issues,
He gives us the courage to move forward
With love and happiness
As He allows our lives to continue.

The Great I Am,
We thank you truly for all that you do
For our single heart beats for the love and joy
We receive from you.

FAVOR

Follow the Lord's Will
Allow Him to lead your way
Value His love for its truly real
Only through Him you can receive the F.O.G.
Reach out to Him, show Him your love,
   for you already have the L.O.G.

F.O.G. (Favor of God)   L.O.G. (Love of God)

THE BLOOD

People have their own perception of what Jesus looks like,
Some say He's black, some say He's white,
If you ask me, I may say I'm color blind;
For it was His Blood
Not the color of His skin
That saved this life of mine.

It was the Blood that ran through the veins
Of a powerful man with many and one powerful name,
Who came, who bled, and who died
So that we all could be saved.

It was the Blood of Jesus that was shed in the
halls of the Praetorium
Where He was mocked and beaten nearly to death,
It was the blood He shed on Calvary
Where in the ninth hour He took His very last breath.

It was the Blood of Jesus that saved us
Not the color of His skin,
It was His Blood
That covers and cleanses us deeply within.

People have their own perception of what Jesus looks like,
Some say He's black, some say He's white,
If you ask me, I may say I'm color blind;
For it was His Blood
Not the color of His skin
That saved this life of mine.

AS YOU MOVE FORWARD

Written By: Demetrai L Johnson
Dedicated To: Katrina Johnson Young
2/2011

There are times in your life where you have to look back
and see how far you have come,
From childhood, to adolescence, to becoming an adult
Looking back at all the obstacles you had to face and overcome.

As you move forward,
Challenges will still be there for you to face every single day,
Family, friends, finances,
Your job, enemies, or self can sometime get in the way.

As you move forward
To pursue the Will of God
Remember, you are not moving forward on your own,
For you have the Almighty Triune God
Who loves, saves, provides, protects, guides, & comforts you;
You are not alone.

As you move forward
Wait on the Lord our God; and take courage
Seek Him first in everything you do,
Continue to pray, love, give and grow in His word
Just as He prays, loves, gives, and grows within you.

As you move forward
Trust in the Lord with all your heart,
Lean not to your own understanding
Shout Glory Hallelujah!
Praise Him in advance
For the over flow of His Blessings.

HE REALLY CARES

Throughout my life there have been heartaches and pains,
Eternal bleeding from the heart is what I would gain.
Tears that run down the face of someone who
wants to love again.

Will it ever happen, I don't know
For it's in the hands of my Lord and Savior,
Who closes and opens my doors.
He's shielding my heart from more shattering cracks, while
fixing the ones already there;
He's making sure I hurt no more
Showing me He really cares.

Words
of
Remembrance

In Loving Memory of My Great Grandmother Mattie Reynolds

Dear Great Grandmamma,

It's me, that girl, some girl, Mildred's kid. Just a memory of how you could never call me by my name.

I also remember how you would rake the yard in the sun while in your 90's while we complained about it being too hot and tired. Whenever we would ask for Kool-Aid you would say **"Those Chaps Don't Need No Kool-Aid To Drink"** Lol… I still laugh at that until this day when I think about you.

I remember when I would have to come and stay the weekend with you to help you out. Especially, when I had to come after celebrating my birthday. I must admit I really didn't want to go due to me being the only kid around sometimes, and the fact that you could never call me by my name. Even though I didn't want to come, I did like the fact that I was able to spend time with you, and to help out.

I remember your big blue eyed yellow cat that I would try to scare due to me not liking cats. Of course he or she would look at me like I'm crazy. Oh well what can I say, I tried.

What I remember most about you is having your birthday party on Sunday's even though it was on another day. To me it was more like a family reunion. Everyone would show up to celebrate your birthday. To see the smile on your face as we sing "Happy Birthday" to you. Also, that serious look on your face when you opened a card with no money in it.

My last memory of you was the night you past away. I came to your room after either a track meet or practice. We all were in your room talking. I was sitting near the open window. I ended up falling asleep. As I was sleep, I felt the cool breeze coming in across the back of my neck. I could hear people talking but I can't remember what was being said. All I remember is that feeling I felt inside of me, as the breeze kept blowing cross my neck. The feeling that I had was about you. I felt that you were going to leave us that night. I was taken home that night to get some sleep due to being really tired from having a long day. I remember being awakened from a deep sleep into a light sleep when my mom and cousin Reggie came home. I heard them talking and that's when I found out that you had passed away.

Grandma, I miss you, and glad that you are in a better place.

Love you Always,
Mildred's kid

In Loving Memory of My Uncle Michael L. Johnson

CRY NO MORE

In special memory of my Beloved Uncle Michael Lee Johnson
October 20, 1955 - June 18, 2005

Cry no more
My Father has called me home
You know our bodies are only temporary,
While our Spirit carries on.

Cry no more
For I'm no longer suffering,
The new life I have now is everlasting,
My body is truly functioning
I can happily say now I'm walking.

Cry no more
For I am happy
Shed no more tears and be glad for me
I made it into the gates of Heaven
My spirit has been set completely free.

Cry no more
Miss me not
For I am still with you
The time will come for us to meet again
If you confess with your mouth, that Jesus is Lord
Believe in your heart that God raised him from the dead, you
will be saved.
And He will surely see you through.

Cry no more
My family and friends
I've made it into the gates of Heaven
The place; where my new life begins.

Dear Uncle Mike,

It's me Tweety. The nick name you gave me when I was little.
I want you to know that you are really missed by your family.
As for me myself, I truly miss you.

Memories of you would pop into my mind, and at times bring tears
to my eyes. I remember growing up how you use to help me with
reading, and my homework. I'm happy to say that I still use the
reading method when I'm helping a kid to read. They may not like it
but hey that's the way I learned and that's the way I plan to teach my
own, if I ever have any.

I remember you helping me study for my driver's exam. Even though it
took me two times to pass. You helped me both times. Thanks!

Uncle Mike, I miss hearing your voice telling me things I need to
know. Then hearing you say; "See what I'm saying".

I miss coming by your home two to three times a week after work to
check up on you and helping you when needed. Cooking dinner
when you haven't done so. Speaking of cooking, I miss your
cooking. That taste of your homemade fries and fried chicken. Also,
you're delicious tasting sweet potatoes. I haven't tasted any like that
yet.

I miss watching the Court shows on television when I get there. I
miss making each other laugh.

Uncle Mike there is one thing I don't miss is your ALLIGATOR
BELT! LOL!

Well Uncle Mike, I must end this letter. I know that I've thanked
you each time you've done something for me. I just want to say it
again.

Thank you for everything you've done for me.

We (your family) love and miss you!

In Loving Memory of Cindy Nicole Stacey Shelton
August 17, 1974 – November 23, 2005

My Dear Sister Cindy,

It's me your little sister. You know the one who use to follow you just about everywhere whenever I came to visit. The one who always wanted to hear you sing.

Sis, I want you to know that I really enjoyed having you as one of my sisters. I miss you dearly.

I miss spending time with you whenever we could. Talking with you and having you sing to me like you use to do when we were little. I remember how I would have you sing "God Has Always Stood By My Side" I must say that there is something about the song that I love. I guess it was the way you sung it.

Well as of today I still sing that song. I sing it better than what I use to sing it. Oh of course not better than you. I remember the day before you took your last breath, I so wanted to sing that song for you. I guess since we were at the hospital I didn't want to get loud.

Now when I sing it, I will think about you. You are the one who introduced me to it. Back then I really didn't understand the song but loved it and started singing it at church (St. Paul Presbyterian). As I grew order and became closer to God, I began to understand what I was singing about. I began to love the song more.

Now I sing it for the Voice of Praise Choir of Silver Mount Missionary Baptist Church. The church where Lincoln C. Lee pastors; you know him as "Poochie".

Sis, I miss your encouraging words. How you would encourage me to stay in God's word. I still have the bible you gave me the year my Uncle Mike died. You wrote in the inside of it "By your Big Sister, Continue to stay in the word and watch how God blesses U.

You gave it to me on June 23, 2005. You also made a plant for my Uncle that same day.

I remember I told you about a dream. I had a dream a year before my Uncle past. I told you that I believe that God was using the dream to prepare me for what was going to happen, I didn't know it. I told you that there was one more person that God was calling home and I didn't know who it was going to be. I knew then it had to be you or my Aunt Brenda Wentz, (my mom's baby sister). I asked you, if you could make my wedding dress for me just in case. You told me that it wasn't going to be you.

On November 23, 2005, you left me here. You were called home to be with Our Heavenly Father. I was hurt and happy for you. Happy knowing that you're no longer suffering. Hurt because I knew you were no longer here to talk with me. To hear you sing with the voice God blessed you with.

Well my sister, I must end here. Just know that we (your brother Antonio and sisters Lisa and I) and the rest of the family miss and love you.

I REMEMBER
(For both Uncle Mike & Big Sister Cindy)

I remember the night when I went to bed
The soft sound of "Didn't You Know" by
Donnie McClurkin playing in reality
I was deeply in my sleep when it started to play in my head.

I began to sing while I was sleeping comfortable in my bed
Holding all the long notes,
As I begin to look ahead.
I saw two smiling faces that didn't look familiar to me
Then I look further up and saw my Savior Jesus Christ
Standing between the gates of Heaven,
Reaching down for me.

Ever since the dream came to me,
I would just think about how wonderful it made me feel
My heart would lighten up
And my face would hold a smile;
To me this dream felt real.

Ever since then the Lord has blessed me in so many ways
He brought me out without a doubt
I owe Him all the praise.

This dream took place in 2004. On June 18, 2005, the true
meaning of the dream was revealed to me. The faces that I saw
were the faces of my Uncle Michael L. Johnson, and my Big
Sister Cindy Nicole Stacey Shelton. They died five months apart.

God was letting me know that He was taking my loved ones to
be with Him. After my Uncle passed away, I knew someone was
next and that it had to be between my Aunt Brenda Wentz, and
my sister Cindy. All three was sick during that time; however, my
Aunt is still with us. THANK YOU GOD!!!

In Loving Memory of Larry Stacey
September 5, 1952 – March 16, 1998

LARRY S

Lord I ask you to take my father,
Larry Stacey under your Heavenly wings,
Amaze him with your presence and bless us with peaceful dreams.
Rise Soul Rise to Our Father's House the Lord up Above,
Rest in Peace Larry Stacey as you depart from the ones you love.
You've left behind four beautiful children & family who
really needs you,
So surround us with your spirit and help us feel it too.

GOODBYE
Written in the memory of Larry Stacey

I remember the day you couldn't say goodbye,
I wasn't mad at you
I knew why.

I held your hand and chest
As you took your last breath,
I was really hoping
That you could be nursed back to health.

As I closed your eyes
A tear ran down your face,
It was the last of many
To leave a trace.

After all of that
I understand why
You couldn't look at us and say goodbye.

DADDY

Daddy
Where were you
When I took my first breath
I don't remember whether
or not you were there.

Daddy
Where were you
When I took my first step
You weren't even around
enough to see me like that.

Daddy
Where were you
When I got the first boo-
boo on my knee
You wasn't there to patch it
up and to say you'll be ok
Now go out and play.

Daddy
Where were you
When I needed you most
With the suffering and pain
I don't deserve nor want.

Well that's the past
But it still hurts me the most
Because all I ever wanted
was for us to be real close.

Yes I was mad because of the
times we've wasted
But we've shared the phrase
"I LOVE YOU"
Every time we saw one
another face to face.

Daddy
As of this year
I know where you're at,
It wasn't your fault
So I'm not mad at that.

Even though Daddy
I still need you now
Your daughter is hurt
Your daughter is down.

Daddy
I lost another love
With you being first
This time it's wasn't to death
For death is much worst.

WATCHING OVER ME WITH GOD

Every time something goes wrong
I seem to think of you
Even though you weren't around for me to turn too.
During my college days
I would sit and wonder
What's missing in my life?
It was you and the fact that things weren't going right.
You wanted to be here to see me get married
Now that you're gone
It will never happen.
I know your looking down on me
Seeing things you shouldn't see
But knowing you are watching over me with God
Makes me feel happy.

In Loving Memory of

Brenda Stacey,
Desiree Stinson
&
Audrey Dixon

In Loving Memory of My Aunt Brenda Stacey
August 20, 1962 – March 12, 2002

THE RAIN TODAY

The rain today was a sign of death. It was my aunt's life, as she took her last breath. In her dream she was running with her brother to the finish line, it took three years and five days to catch-up, for she was left behind. Now, she has caught up with him on this day and time. She died the same month as my dad; whom I still mourn from time to time.

In Loving Memory of Desiree Stinson
July 26, 2006 – August 6, 2006

DESIREE
Written: August 30, 2006

During the time we spent together on earth,

Eleven days was all I needed… including the

Seven months of refuge before my birth.

I enjoyed every moment you held me in your loving arms,

Rejoice for me my loving mother for I'm now safe from harm.

Everlasting Love has called me home, to free me
  from suffering.. so

Everyday mommy when you think of me, look up to
  God's beautiful skies above with the sign of love, and
  know that I love you.

This was written as a message from
Desiree to her mother Jayvette Stinson,

AN ANGEL WHO WAS CALLED HOME
Written: 07/5/2013

Audrey,
You're an Angel, who was called home,
Leaving behind your loving sweet spirit
Reminding us that you're not completely gone.

You are a God fearing Angel who has walked this earth
Carrying such a lovely, beautiful, and giving heart,
Your honesty, intelligence, and talented ways also played a part.

Audrey,
You're an Angel who was called home
To a place we all would love to be,
You're in Heaven, your new home,
Where you can enjoy your new life joyful and free.

WEEP FOR ME NOT

Note: This poem is for my Obituary

Weep for me not for Our Father has called me home,
Remember me in your hearts so you won't feel alone.

Weep not for me for it was my time,
It is my body that's being laid to rest
Not this lovely spirit of mine.

Weep for me not for Our Father has called me home,
Wipe away the streams of your salty water tears
For I rather be in Heaven then to live in a world that's
gone wrong.

Weep not for me for it was my time
Put a smile on your face
Reminisce on the good times
That can never be replaced.

Weep for me not my family and friends,
I love you all and would love to recommend
Accept the Lord Jesus Christ in your life as your Savior,
And allow the Holy Spirit to dwell within.

My message to all: I love you all... When you think of me,
think of the good times. Think about Peanut Butter &
Jelly... Ice Cream & Cake. LOL!! If you don't know what
I'm talking about, then ask the person beside you.

ABOUT THE AUTHOR

Demetrai L. Johnson, a native of Charlotte, is the middle child on both sides of her family. She graduated from Johnson C. Smith University with a Bachelor's of Arts Degree in Communications with the focus on Television Productions.

Demetrai has been blessed with the gift of writing and other talents. She discovered her talent during her elementary years with writing poetry, her first children story ("John the Talking Dog") and first rap song ("Yum Yum Bubble Gum"). Ever since then, she has been writing poetry, songs, and other things that are an inspiration to her.

Demetrai also enjoys singing, acting, working in front as well as behind cameras, Photography, and helping others.

www.ingramcontent.com/pod-product-compliance
Lightning Source LLC
Chambersburg PA
CBHW060102050426
42448CB00011B/2595